7-4-79

know the game Weight Lifting

Contents

101

FOREWORD

From the time of man's advent on earth, the urge to prove his superiority over fellow man has been a strong driving force. Superiority in the form of strength has been easy to satisfy since the dawn of man, for natural means were always at hand—stones, rocks, tree branches and trunks. It is possible to suppose that the lifting of weights, with wrestling and running, were among man's earliest means of measuring superiority.

When Baron Pierre de Coubertin's dream of reviving the ancient Olympic Games came to fruition in 1896, weightlifting was a necessary part of the programme. Control of weightlifting this day is under the jurisdiction of the International Weightlifting Federation, with over 100 countries affiliated. Control is exercised in this country by the British Amateur Weight Lifters Association. Scotland and Wales, affiliated to the British Association, have a large measure of autonomy.

There are nine weightlifting classes accepted for international competition, ranging from flyweight to super heavyweight. Nine competitors from each participating country is the maximum allowed for the Olympic and Commonwealth Games, World and European Championships, and all the other regional games, African, Asian, Central American and Caribbean, Mediterranean, Pan American, S.E.A.P. and South Pacific. As will be seen, the practice of weightlifting as a competitive sport is global.

The use of weights goes far beyond competition; weight training is a basic part of the training for many other sports and one has only to think of those athletes, from a variety of sports, showing proficiency in the use of weights, featured from time to time in television programmes.

A National Coach was appointed in the early 50's with the aid of a Government grant, to train instructors to impart the necessary fundamental knowledge of the body at all ages, to reject the unsuitable, to var exercises and to meet the requirements of varying physical conditions. This took not days, but month and years. This Coaching Scheme, as it was known bore fruit, with the result that today the Association i its National Coaching Advisor, National Coach, an staff coaches, has perhaps the most informed of a coaching cadres in sport in this country, being con stantly invited to staff coaching clinics world wide Below the level of Staff Coach the Association ha scores of instructors and coaches preparing to take th stiff higher examinations. If successful they join an elit cadre.

A Schoolboys' Association has been formed t look after and promote the interests of this all-importan group. The establishment of a Teachers Awar Certificate ensures that they receive the expe supervision and tuition that is a basic tenet of th Association's thinking and practice on weightliftin and weight training at all levels.

H. W. Hartnall,
Chairman and President
British Amateur Weight Lifters Asso

INTRODUCTION

Weightlifting must be one of the oldest sports known to mankind. Tests of strength have always been a challenge to young men throughout history and all civilisations have their legends associated with great feats of power. It is a long way, however, from the exploits of the past ages to the modern strength athlete of today, involved in an exciting and dynamic sporting activity.

This book will introduce you to the sport of modern weightlifting. It will explain the technique of the two lifts that have been selected, by the International Weightlifting Federation, as the most suitable tests of athletic power, and will explain how to train to reach high standards in these lifts.

The two lifts that we shall be concerned with are the Two Hands Snatch and the Two Hands Clean and Jerk. These are the lifts which are used in all competitions controlled by the International Weightlifting Federation, and it is upon the results achieved on these lifts that the World, Olympic and National Champions are decided. Competitions, however, begin at much more modest levels and the beginner will find championships designed to challenge his abilities and progress at all grades.

The sport of weightlifting is truly international, and at its topmost level provides the participant with the opportunity to achieve the highest sporting honours. For those however who do not achieve these heights, it is a fine club activity which can be followed for many

Fig. 1

years, giving great satisfaction. Remember as you read these pages that the sport will demand that you become an all-round athlete, and that at whatever level you compete the qualities of great strength and speed, mastery of technique, physical fitness, courage and, above all, dedication are essential ingredients of success.

EQUIPMENT

Apparatus

Weightlifting is performed on a barbell with disc weights which range from 25 kgs down to one and a half kgs, so that a fully comprehensive range of poundages can be made up. The barbell can revolve within its own end sleeves to facilitate easier lifting, and is knurled to provide a good gripping surface.

All lifts in competition must be performed on a platform measuring four by four metres, and these are made of solid wood with rubber insets where discs and the bar rest.

In addition to the barbell the lifter often uses dumbbells in his training. These are miniature barbells to be used in each hand and are generally made up in pairs of the same weight. Squat stands are also essential. These are height-adjustable stands that the bar can be rested upon during the performance of heavy leg and overhead exercises used in training. A heavy bench, preferably with an adjustable back, is an important part of the basic apparatus as again certain essential exercises are performed on this apparatus.

This apparatus, especially the barbell, can be very expensive. Very few people own such materials, but all good clubs will have a fully comprehensive range of lifting apparatus and weights.

Fig. 2

PERSONAL EQUIPMENT

Perhaps the most important part of a weightlifter's equipment is his boots. These must provide a flat, stable contact with the floor to give maximum balance. These are specially manufactured for the purpose and are the first item that the lifter should buy. A tracksuit is also very important as this is the garment in which the lifter will do most of his training. The best quality that you can afford will pay dividends, and it should be fleece lined to provide a warm covering so that the lifter does not chill between lifts.

For competition there is a special costume or leotard. This should be of one plain colour and can be worn with a T-shirt with short sleeves. Club or national insignia may be worn with this costume.

For those who feel the need, a belt may be worn but this may not exceed ten cms in width. All personal equipment as worn on the lifting platform in competitions is subject to check to ensure that it conforms to the International Regulations. These regulations are strictly adhered to at all times.

Many lifters now provide themselves with extra general training clothes and a pair of training shoes for running and fitness work.

Remember that at all times it is essential to keep yourself warm. You will be working hard and lifting heavy weights. Look after your personal equipment and keep it thoroughly clean and in good repair.

Fig. 3

2054111

5

GENERAL COMPETITION AND RULES

Weightlifting Competitions

Competitions are held on the Snatch and Clean and Jerk, and the lifter is allowed three attempts on each lift. The best attempts on each of the two lifts are then added together to give a total. The lifter with the best total is declared the winner. In the case of two lifters having the same total at the end of the competition, the lifter with the lighter bodyweight will be declared the winner. All competitors will be weighed-in during one hour, a quarter of an hour prior to the start of the competition.

The lifts will be judged by three Referees, and the general running of the competition will also be their responsibility.

The bodyweight categories are as follows—

1. Fly weight . . . . . up to 52 kg
2. Bantam weight . . . up to 56 kg
3. Feather weight . . . up to 60 kg
4. Light weight . . . . up to 67·5 kg
5. Middle weight . . . up to 75 kg
6. Light heavy weight . . up to 82·5 kg
7. Middle heavy weight . . up to 90 kg
8. Heavy weight . . . up to 110 kg
9. Super heavy weight . . over 110 kg

General Rules for the Lifts

THE TWO HANDS SNATCH. The bar shall be placed horizontally in front of the lifter's legs. It shall be gripped, palms downwards, and pulled in a single movement from the ground to the full extent of the arms vertically above the head, whilst either 'Splitting' or bending the legs. The bar shall pass in a continuous movement along the body of which no part other than the feet may touch the ground during the execution of the lift. The weight which has been lifted must be maintained in the final motionless position, the arms and legs extended, the feet on the same line, until the referee's signal to replace the bar on the platform. The turning over of the wrists must not take place until the bar has passed the top of the lifter's head. The lifter may recover in his own time, either from a 'Split' or a 'Squat'.

THE TWO HANDS CLEAN AND JERK.

PART 1   THE CLEAN.

The bar shall be placed horizontally in front of the lifter's legs. It shall be gripped, palms downwards, and brought in a single movement from the ground to the shoulders, while either 'splitting' or bending the legs. The bar must not touch the chest before the final position. It shall then rest on the

Fig. 4

clavicles, or on the chest, or on the arms fully bent. The feet shall be returned to the same line, legs straight, before performing the Jerk. The lifter may make this recovery in his own time.

PART 2   THE JERK.

Bend the legs and extend them as well as the arms, so as to bring the bar to the full stretch of the arms vertically extended.

Return the feet to the same line, arms and legs extended, and await the referee's signal to replace the bar on the platform.

In both the Snatch and the Clean and Jerk, the referee's signal shall be given as soon as the lifter becomes absolutely motionless in all parts of the body.

For the full details of all other rules controlling all aspects of Weightlifting, you are advised to study the B.A.W.L.A. Handbook and the I.W.F. Rule book.

THE STARTING POSITION

The lifter places his insteps under the bar with his feet hip-width apart and his toes pointing forward. He should feel his weight evenly over the base of all the foot. Keeping his back flat, but not vertical, he bends his legs, lowering himself down until he is able to grip the barbell. His shoulders are kept slightly in front of the bar and his arms are straight and rotated outwards at the elbow joint. The hips are higher than the knees, and the head is comfortably up with the eyes looking down and forward. In the Clean and Jerk the arms should be approximately shoulder-width apart, but in the Snatch the grip will be wider and this will result in the body being closer to the thighs.

Fig. 5

THE SQUAT SNATCH

Fig. 6

Figure 6

The feet are approximately hip-width apart. The back is flat but not vertical, and the shoulders are slightly in front of the bar. The arms are straight and the elbows are turned out from the body to ensure a more vertical pull. The width of grip for the Snatch is determined by measuring the distance from elbow joint to elbow joint across the back when the arms are raised horizontally. This distance is then marked on the bar. The hands are then spaced so that the marks lie between the first and second fingers.

Fig. 7

Fig. 8

Fig. 9

Figure 7

As the bar comes off the floor, it is eased slightly in towards the shins, to bring the centre of the load over the centre of the base. This will maintain balance. Good balance will ensure that maximum force can be exerted throughout the lift. The shoulders are kept forward and the arms are straight.

Figure 8

The shoulders are well forward and the bar has travelled back as far as it should go. The arms are quite straight and the bar passes the knees and lower part of the thighs; the lifter will force his hips inwards and upwards towards the bar.

Figure 9

The hips are now being forced towards the bar. This must be a very determined action. The head is almost vertical over the bar and the lifter is still attempting to keep his shoulders in a pulling position over the bar. He is aiming for maximum upward extension of the body.

Fig. 10

Fig. 11

Fig. 12

Figure 10

This is a key position in all lifts. The body is high on the toes, fully extended with the shoulders elevated. The feet are just about to leave the ground. The arms are still straight and the lifter should not attempt to bend them until this leg, hip and back extension and shoulder elevation nears completion.

Figure 11

As the feet leave the ground both they and the knees are turned outwards and jumped apart. The bar will still be rising on the momentum imparted to it by the correct extension of the body. The lifter must direct the hip region downwards and forwards in order to be able to maintain a vertical trunk position when he lands under the bar.

Figure 12

The lifter approaches the final receiving position beneath the bar by simultaneously performing the following movements: the bar is rotated within its own axis so that the heel of the hand is ready to drive the bar vertically upwards; the knees are opened and the hip region is pushed forwards and downwards so that the lifter can 'sit in and sit up'.

Figure 13

Here we see the lifter in the final receiving position. This is the lowest possible position beneath the bar. The bar is held above the head and shoulders, and over the centre of the base and the upper two-thirds of the trunk are vertical. This is a very strong position for holding heavy weights.

To recover from the final low position of balance, the lifter eases his head through the arms and simultaneously lifts the hips upwards. The arms remain vertical but there is a slight forward inclination of the trunk as the legs extend. The knees should be kept apart during this movement. On reaching the upright position the feet should be stepped back to hip-width and in line to complete the lift.

Fig. 13

Fig. 14

Fig. 15

Fig. 16

Fig. 17

THE SPLIT SNATCH

Figure 18

The feet are hip-width apart, pointing as near fore and aft as is comfortable. The back is flat and the shoulders are slightly in front of the bar. The arms are straight, head up, eyes looking to the front. The hands are approximately 30 inches apart. The bar is over the insteps and the weight of the body is evenly distributed over all of the base of the foot.

Fig. 18

Fig. 19

Fig. 20

Fig. 21

Figure 19

As the bar is lifted from the platform, ease it back slightly so that as it passes the knees it is over the centre of the foot. Lead the pull with the head and shoulders, driving strongly with the legs. The shins will now move backwards, permitting the bar to move vertically as it passes the knees. Keep the head and shoulders forward and the arms straight.

Figure 20

As the bar passes the knees stay evenly on both feet and drive high and upwards with the head, simultaneously forcing the hips forward and upward towards the bar. Lift the shoulders but try to keep them over the bar as long as possible. Reach as high as you can on the toes of both feet.

Figure 21

Having reached the greatest height possible on the toes, both feet must leave the ground at exactly the same time, splitting fore and aft. The body will travel forwards and downwards under the bar.

Figure 22

As the bar passes the top of the head the wrists are turned over so that the bar can be driven vertically with the heel of the hand. Simultaneously the front knee must be pushed forward over the front foot as the body is lowered under the bar.

Figure 23

This is called the Receiving Position. The lifter is now correctly balanced under the bar, with the bar, shoulders and hip joints in one vertical line. Remember, balance means control. To recover from this position, allow the bar to tip back slightly at the same time using the rear leg as a prop. Push with the front leg and move the front foot a few inches back. Now step the rear foot into line with the front foot to arrive at the finishing position of the lift.

Fig. 22

Fig. 23

Fig. 24

THE SQUAT CLEAN

Fig. 25

Fig. 26

Fig. 27

Figure 25

In this illustration the bar has just left the floor. The back is flat and the head and shoulders are slightly in front of the bar. The bar is gripped with the palms downwards and the hands about shoulder-width apart. The arms are straight. The drive comes from the legs, and as they straighten the bar is eased back into the shins to keep it over the centre of the base and to maintain balance.

Figure 26

As the legs straighten the bar should be at knee height.

The shoulders are slightly forward of the bar and the arms, rotated outwards at the elbows, remain straight. The combined weight of body and bar must be evenly distributed over the feet.

Figure 27

As the bar passes the knees and lower thighs (Fig. 26), the hips must be thrust forward and upward towards the bar. The chest must be kept high and a very strong effort must be made to drive the body upwards. The shoulders are elevated strongly and the arms are still straight.

Fig. 28

Figure 28
Having reached a position of maximum upward extension, the lifter must now move down and under the bar to be able to catch it on his chest. The position of the trunk, as achieved in the extension, must be maintained. The feet are turned outwards and jumped apart, and the knees are also turned outwards. The arms now bend as the lifter pulls hard on the bar to accelerate his descent.

Fig. 29

Figure 29
As the feet come to land, the lifter must keep his knees turned out, and place his hips close between his heels. The bar is rotated on its own axis, and the elbows must be brought down and under the bar to secure it on the chest. The speed of descent should be controlled by a braking action of the legs.

Fig. 30

Figure 30

This is the receiving position for the Squat Clean. The hips are close between the heels with the feet and knees turned outwards. This permits an upright trunk. The elbows must be held up high and away from the knees. The bar is resting on the shoulders and clavicles.

To recover from this low position the trunk is tilted slightly forward, keeping the elbows high. This action will lift the seat and begin the straightening of the legs at the knees. The lifter, keeping his knees turned out all the time, must force his way up to an erect position. The feet should then be stepped in to hip-width prior to the Jerk.

Fig. 31

THE SPLIT CLEAN

Fig. 32   Fig. 33   Fig. 34

Figure 32

In this position the bar has just left the floor. The back is flat and the head and shoulders are slightly in advance of the bar. The bar is held with the hands approximately shoulder-width apart and the arms are straight. As the legs straighten, the bar is eased back into the shins to keep it over the centre of the base and to maintain balance.

Figure 33

As the legs straighten, the bar should be at knee height. Maintain the shoulders in front of the bar and the arms, elbows rotated outwards, remain straight. The combined weight of body and bar must be evenly distributed over all the feet.

Figure 34

As the bar passes the knees and lower thighs (Fig. 33), the hips must be thrust forward and upward towards the bar. The chest must be kept high and the arms are still straight.

Fig. 35

Fig. 36

Figure 36

This is referred to as the position of Maximum Upward Extension. It is a key position in the technique of all cleaning movements. The legs and back are fully extended and the bodyweight is travelling over the ball of both feet. With very heavy weights the arms will remain straight, but every effort must be made to elevate the shoulders and impart maximum momentum to the bar.

Fig. 37

Fig. 38

Figure 37

From the position of Maximum Extension, the lifter must split both feet from the ground at exactly the same time. The upright position of the trunk must be maintained as he drops down and forward under the bar. This movement downwards can be accelerated by pulling on the bar after the feet have left the ground.

Figure 38

The feet will land together and the downward and forward action of the body is maintained by pushing the hips towards the front ankle and the knee over the foot. The upright position of the trunk is maintained and the bar, hands and forearms are rotated to secure the bar on the chest. This is the Receiving Position.

To recover from this low receiving position the rear leg is used as a rotating prop from the rear toe, whilst the bar is tipped slightly backwards during the vigorous extension of the front leg. As the front leg nears extension the front foot is moved backwards a few inches. The rear leg raises the body and weight forwards and upwards so that both feet can be placed in line to complete this part of the lift prior to the Jerk

Fig. 39

Fig. 40

THE JERK

Figure 41
The 'get set' for the Jerk must be well balanced, with the weight equally distributed over all of the feet. The elbows are held up to secure the bar on the chest. Slight adjustments are permitted to the position of the bar on the chest, following the Clean, for comfort.

Figure 42
Maintaining the upright position of the trunk, chest high and elbows up, the body is lowered vertically by bending the knees. The depth of this knee bend is governed by maintaining the feet flat on the ground and keeping the trunk vertical. Correct procedure in this part of the movement is most important in correct Jerking technique.

Figure 43
From the position in *Fig.* 42, thrust the trunk upwards, keeping it in a vertical position throughout. This should bring you high on the balls of both feet. Drive upwards viciously with both arms and split both feet, making sure that they come off the ground at exactly the same time. As the bar flies upwards, keep the chest high, and aim to place the upper arms vertically above the shoulder joints.

Figure 44

The split landing position should be high, providing firm support for the weight. The chest must be kept high to provide the best shoulder movement so that bar, shoulders and hips are in a direct line of support under the bar. To recover from the Split Receiving position, tilt the bar slightly backwards and, using the rear leg as a prop, step the front foot a few inches back. Keeping the chest high at all times, step the rear foot forward into line with the front foot.

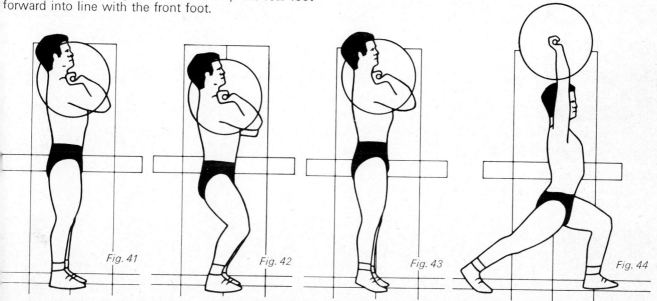

Fig. 41   Fig. 42   Fig. 43   Fig. 44

ASSISTANCE EXERCISES

High Pull up

STARTING POSITION

Feet hip-width apart, insteps under the bar. Bend the knees and hips and grip the bar with the knuckles to the front, hands shoulder-width apart. The hips should be higher than the knees and the back flat with the shoulders slightly in advance of the bar. This is called the 'Get set' position, Fig. 45.

MOVEMENT

Lift with the legs maintaining the position of the back and head. As the bar passes the knees force the hips forwards and upwards, reaching for a position of maximum upward extension as in Fig. 46. Lower the bar to the starting position by bending the legs.

BREATHING

Breathe in on the effort of lifting the bar and out when lowering.

PURPOSE

To build real power in the legs, back, shoulders and grip.

This exercise may be performed with a wide grip as for the Snatch.

Fig. 45

Fig. 46

Jerk Balance

STARTING POSITION

Assume the position in Fig. 47. Make sure that the weight is evenly distributed over both feet and that the trunk is nearly vertical. The bar should rest solidly on the chest.

MOVEMENT

Bend both knees quickly, straightening the legs, and at the same time drive upwards with the arms and shoulders. As the bar clears the top of the head, dip the body by bending the knees to receive the bar in position, Fig. 48. Straighten both legs, then lower to starting position, Fig. 47.

BREATHING

Breathe in as the bar is driven overhead, and out as it is lowered.

PURPOSE

To develop the skill and timing in Jerking weights overhead and to develop power in this movement.

Fig. 47

Fig. 48

Split Snatch Balance Press

STARTING POSITION

Assume the position in Fig. 49, making sure you are perfectly balanced before you attempt to make your movement.

MOVEMENT

From this position, keeping the feet firmly in the same position, quickly bend and stretch the legs. At the same time drive the bar slightly forwards and upwards with the arms. Now dip the body as the bar passes the forehead, lowering into the position shown in Fig. 50. This position is known as the Receiving Position.

Note that the trunk is vertical and the knee of the front leg is pushed well forward over the ankle. Try to sit on the forward heel without the rear knee touching the floor.

BREATHING

Breathe as freely as possible.

PURPOSE

To assist in teaching the Split Style Snatch, and to develop the quality of mobility, co-ordination, power and confidence essential in learning this fine athletic lift.

Fig. 49

Fig. 50

26

Squat Snatch Balance Press

STARTING POSITION

Assume the position as in Fig. 51, making sure that the feet are turned outwards.

MOVEMENT

Dip the body by maintaining both legs to lower the bar a few inches. Immediately rebound from this shallow knee-bend by extending the legs and arms to send the bar upwards. Drop under the weight as in Fig. 52, by bending the knees into a full squat. It is important to force the knees outwards and to keep the trunk upright.

BREATHING

Breathe as freely as possible.

PURPOSE

To assist in teaching the Squat Style Snatch, and to develop the qualities of mobility, co-ordination, power and confidence essential in learning this fine athletic lift.

Fig. 51

Fig. 52

Front Squats

Fig. 53

Fig. 54

STARTING POSITION

Load the barbell on the squat stands. Grip the bar, bend the knees and raise the bar clear of the stands. Step back from the stands. Place the feet hip-width apart with the toes turned out. Keep the elbows high throughout the movement, Fig. 53.

MOVEMENT

Lower the body into position, Fig. 54. Vigorously extend the legs and, keeping the chest high and th back flat and upright, return to the standing position

BREATHING

Breathe out as you bend the knees, and in as yo rise to the standing position.

PURPOSE

Mainly to develop the muscles on the front of th thigh and the hip muscles.

Split Squats

STARTING POSITION

Take up the position shown in Fig. 55. Make sure that your balance is perfect before attempting the movement.

MOVEMENT

Lower the body and the weight from position Fig. 55 to that in Fig. 56 by bending both legs. Note how the forward knee is in advance of the forward foot. Straighten both legs to starting position.

BREATHING

Breathe as freely as possible during the exercise.

PURPOSE

To build power and mobility in the legs in the Receiving position employed in the Split Clean.

Fig. 55

Fig. 56

Power Cleans with Barbell

STARTING POSITION

Assume position in Fig. 57. The legs are well bent but the back is flat.

MOVEMENT

Extend the legs and back vigorously, bringing the arms into action as the bar passes the knees, finishing in the position in Fig. 58.

BREATHING

Breathe in as you lift, and out as you lower the bar to the starting position.

PURPOSE

To develop all-round body power.

Fig. 57

Fig. 58

Squat

Deep Knee Bend

STARTING POSITION

Feet are comfortably apart, normally hip-width and with the toes turned out slightly, with the bar resting across the upper back, Fig. 59.

MOVEMENT

Bend the knees and squat down as low as in Fig. 60, gently rebound out of this position and rise strongly by lifting the head; at the same time strongly straightening the legs.

LOW POSITION

In most cases it is neither necessary nor advisable to go lower than in Fig. 60. The back is kept flat but not vertical. This position elevates the ribs and has a stretching effect on the thorax, which encourages chest growth.

BREATHING

Fill the lungs, bend the knees, breathe out just as you reach the low position. Breathe in as you rise.

PURPOSE

To develop the legs, back and chest, and to improve the condition of the respiratory and circulatory systems.

Fig. 59

Fig. 60

31

Sets and Repetitions

The amount of work that one requires to do is broken up into sets of a required number of repetitions, for example: if a lifter decided that he needs to perform thirty repetitions of an exercise his choice would be between the development of endurance or strength. For endurance he might complete the thirty repetitions in one set without any rest. This would mean that the weight would have to be light. On the other hand, as one of the main objectives of weightlifting training is to develop strength, the resistance handled must be increased. Now he could not perform one set of thirty, so the exercise is performed over three sets of ten repetitions, or six sets of five or at more advanced levels when the resistance is very heavy—ten sets of three. This is known as the Set System of Training.

Schedules and Plans

Schedules are the plans of work and layout of the exercises, and the sets and repetitions to be followed. Planning these schedules is really a task to be undertaken between the lifter and his coach, and progress will depend upon these plans. However, certain basic ideas can govern the construction of a schedule especially for the beginner: for example, the beginner must learn the exercises and the movements to be mastered and so, in order to build up patterns of movements, the repetitions must be fairly high. A schedule may be as follows, and training should be at least three and, preferably, four times a week.

Monday	Tuesday	Thursday	Friday
Snatch	Clean & Jerk	As for	As for
Power Clean	Snatch Balance	Monday	Tuesday
High Pulls	High Pulls		
(Clean Grip)	(Snatch Grip)		
Back Squats	Front or Split		
	Squats		

Much attention to technique must be applied in these schedules.

All these exercises should be performed for five sets of five repetitions each, and the weights used will be governed by the following: for the Snatch 50% of the lifter's own bodyweight, for the Clean and Jerk add 10 kgs (22 lbs) to this figure. All the assistance exercises can operate on training weights in the range of 70%–100% of Snatch and Clean and Jerk.

Such a programme could be followed over four to six weeks and then poundages will be increased with consequent changes in sets and repetitions. Should any weaknesses in muscle groups or in technique become apparent the coach will adjust the exercise programme accordingly.

Long-term planning is important, and it is essential to select competitions in which you hope to do well and to plan your training so that you reach a peak of performance at that time. Good coaching is essential in making these preparations.

All plans must take into consideration the following qualities, as possession of these will make up the basis of success.

TRAINING METHODS
OBJECTIVES

Strength

The development of strength is dependent on overcoming great resistance through the muscular system. This will involve the lifter in handling progressively heavier weights in his training and thereby developing this quality. The training programme and exercises are arranged with this end in view.

Speed

This quality involves the muscle acting against a resistance to produce fast movement at the joints above the normal. Speed is dependent to a great degree on muscular strength to activate the joints against the resistance in the shortest possible time. Even though the heavy resistances handled in weightlifting reduce the speed of movement, the lifter must harness all his mental powers to 'get the weight moving as fast as possible'.

Power

Power is the end-product of strength and speed. A very strong man can be slow in his movement, and a very fast man comparatively weak in the weightlifting sense, but the successful weightlifter must develop great power. This means that he is strong and fast moving.

Balance and Mobility

The techniques of weightlifting, as you will have seen, require that the lifter moves with great speed into unusual receiving positions, and at the same time must control and support a very heavy resistance. This requires that he has a keen sense of balance and the necessary mobility in the joint complexes to achieve these steady and controlled positions. Certain exercises help to develop balance and mobility and, of course, strength in the final receiving positions.

Courage

There is no doubt that the successful weightlifter must be 'brave' in the face of the maximum poundages that he may have to attempt to win a competition or set new records. This quality is best developed through successful training and the knowledge that all the necessary qualities of strength, speed, fitness and mastery of techniques have been thoroughly covered.

Fitness

Whatever physical activity you are involved in, be it running or swimming, major games, indoor activities or weightlifting, the greater the degree of basic physical fitness that can be developed and maintained, the

Fig. 61

greater the possibility of success in the activity. The weightlifter does not require the endurance fitness of the long-distance runner, but the systems of heart, lungs and circulation must be highly efficient to ensure that he can train hard and recover quickly. Much of his fitness work will include speed work and flexibility training. This will involve short sprinting, standing high and long jumps, and simple gymnastic exercises to ensure full range of mobility in all the joint complexes. This, coupled with his normal weightlifting training, should ensure a standard of physical fitness which will help to bring the lifter to a high level of performance.

Fig. 62

THE COMPETITION PROGRAMME

Competitions are organised at all levels from club to world and Olympic Games. Most lifters begin with club or county championships and, depending on how well they do in these, they may be invited to the divisional championships. These competitions are for lifters from a large area of the country, usually comprising several counties, and it is at these that the better lifters try to qualify, by achieving certain set totals, for the British Championships. British Championships are held for schoolboys, juniors, under 23's and senior lifters, and qualifying totals are set for all these. The B.A.W.L.A. have a special selection committee whose task it is to select the best lifters at all British Championships, for international, home and away matches, and for the Commonwealth and Olympic Games. Standards for these competitons are very high indeed, and those selected will have had many years of hard work behind them.

In addition to the competition programme there are several schemes in operation at all times, so that a lifter may have targets to achieve. The main ones are the Certificate of Merit in which a lifter may, after achieving certain standards, be awarded certificates; the B.A.W.L.A. National Grading Scheme with the top level being the Gold award, and a similar award specially designed for schoolboys. Full details of these and other schemes can be obtained from the General Secretary.

Fig. 63

WEIGHTLIFTING SAFETY FOR PUPILS AND COMPETITORS

The use of weights as a means of developing strength and power is very old indeed. Weight training, i.e. strength and muscle-building, is a very worthwhile end in itself. Strength is respectable. It assists in the development of skill acquisition, and is an important aspect of any physical fitness programme. The sport of weightlifting is exciting, requiring great strength, speed, mental control, fitness and courage and mastery of technique. Many of the world's greatest athletes employ progressive resistance principles in their training.

Weights, however, are impartial apparatus—they make no distinction between beginners or champions. Their use requires careful thought. The skills of the activity must be learnt very carefully. Poor technique, reckless advancement of poundages, irresponsible behaviour, can cause accidents. Listen to your coach or teacher. Apply the correct training principles, respect the limitations of each individual. Get your thinking right. Do it before you start to train.

People say some unkind things about athletes who do not think and so get hurt. 'Don't worry he is all muscle, especially the head' . . . 'He is as strong as an ox, and almost as clever' . . . 'That was lucky Joe you'd have been in real trouble if you'd landed anywhere other than on your head'. Of course, an injury may result from somebody else not thinking, but if you think and behave responsibly you will never hurt yourself or anybody else. Consider the following . .

1. Confidence should not be confused with recklessness; the former is built on knowledge, the latter on ignorance. The only impression reckless weight training makes is on the floor.

2. Although weight training and weightlifting are great fun because you can see and take pride in the progress you are making, to become an expert still takes time—time spent on understanding and mastering each step before moving on to the next. Don't try to run before you can walk.

3. Before trying the next exercise or training plans and schedules, get and follow advice from your teacher or coach. The teacher's or coach's job is to ensure that all the experiences you will have from the use of weights will be pleasant ones.

4. Never train alone, always have one stand-in at each end of the bar. They should know what you are going to do and when.

5. Keep to your schedule of exercises. Do not advance to poundages without your coach's advice. Do not sacrifice correct body position for poundage.

6. Do not try to keep up with others who may seem to be making more rapid progress than yourself. Train at your own level and within your own capabilities. You will make progress.

7. Horseplay and practical jokes can be very dangerous. If you are not getting enough fun out of serious weightlifting work, it's a poor programme. Wear firm training shoes and warm clothing.

8. Check all apparatus before use and after each exercise. Check collars. Make sure they are firmly secured. Make sure all bars are evenly loaded. Concentrate and be safety conscious.

9. When you are ready for competition lifting it will require that you have followed a sound training programme. Technique must be mastered. Strength and Power building must be developed steadily. Your success in competition will depend upon a controlled and progressive approach to training.

WEIGHTLIFTING SAFETY FOR TEACHERS AND COACHES

Every teacher wants to prevent accidents in Physical Education. Accident victims may suffer physical and psychological injury and distress with impaired future happiness. The P.E. programme may be cut back and all sorts of restrictions introduced. Teachers, coaches and authorities may also suffer stress and loss by being sued for negligence and damages if students are injured whilst using defective equipment; if there was inadequate supervision; if reasonable care was not exercised by the teacher.

To protect your pupils, your employers, your programme, your budget, YOURSELF—give full consideration to the recommendations set out below:

General Physical Education

1. Have all equipment inspected regularly. Report in writing all deficiences in apparatus, mats, floor surfaces, rigs, equipment, etc., to your superior. Don't use until put right. Get the best equipment and keep in good condition.

2. Make sure you have taught all the necessary skills, including safety procedures, before requiring students to exercise them in game, class or competition situations.

3. Get medical approval before putting an injured student back into game, class or competition activity. Get and follow medical advice.
4. Beginners need special teaching and supervision. A champion trying out an entirely new skill is a beginner at that skill. Supervision means being there when needed.
5. Fatigue often precedes accidents. Students must be fit, at the time, for the work to be attempted. A tired pupil is often accident prone.

Weight Training and Lifting

In addition to the above also—keep the apparatus locked up unless at least THREE people want to use it.

1. Ensure that your layout for the different exercises in the Weight Training area is carefully planned. Bar bells should not be too close to each other. Use mats under the weights. Transport of Equipment requires great care. Do not permit horseplay.
2. Check the bar bells, stands, benches, dumbells, etc., carefully before use. Make sure all collars are tight and bar bells evenly loaded. Check each time apparatus comes out and after every set. Your responsibility.
3. Only train in an area where the floor is even, firm and non-slip. Do not permit pupils to train in bare feet. Balance in progressive resistance training is very important.
4. Check and service your equipment regularly. It's good insurance.
5. Know WHY and when to teach specific exercises,

as well as how. Good intentions are no excuse for ignorance. Attend an official coaching course.
6. Make sure that stand-ins (two) are used for all exercises—one each side of the bar bell ready to assist. Teach all pupils how to stand-in and catch. See stand-in knows when and how to help.
7. Ensure that pupil does not attempt limit poundages too soon. Too great a weight = bad body position = accident.
8. Teach exercises carefully. Ensure strict exercise principles are employed at all times. Every pupil must advance at his own level.
9. Use only token resistance during exercise learning phase. When muscle groups are weak they lack control. Lack of muscular control can lead to injury. Proceed with caution and always with careful supervision.
10. Correct breathing on all lifts must be taught. Apply correct training principles.
11. Encourage the use of warm clothing to train in, and fast training procedure to avoid 'local chilling' of muscles. Employ correct training principles.
12. Before driving your pupils to advanced training schedules or too early competitions, get you motives clear. Unless the well being and safety of the performers comes above personal vanity and ambition it could be a dangerous programme. Integrity.
13. Display this notice in the gymnasium and ensure all students are familiar with the recommendations. Have your rules and enforce them. Stay in charge.

B.A.W.L.A.

Schoolboys' Weightlifting Awards

The scheme is designed as a progressive incentive for schoolboys starting weight-training and eventually moving on to weightlifting. The examiner for all grades is the boy's normal teacher or coach. Certificates for all grades are free.

Bronze Award. To qualify a boy must have practised weight-training regularly to the satisfaction of his teacher for not less than six weeks.

Silver Award. This is obtained by achieving certain standards on the International lifts of Snatch and Clean and Jerk. The total needed on these lifts for the Silver Award should equal at least $1\frac{1}{2}$ the boy's own bodyweight.

The Gold Award. The total needed to achieve the Gold standard should equal at least double the boy's own bodyweight.

All boys participating in these award schemes should be members of the B.A.W.L.A. Badges and certificates can be obtained from the Officials of the Schools Association.

Full details of the Coaching Award for School Teachers can be obtained from the B.A.W.L.A. Coaching Secretary.

Conclusion

It is hoped that this book will encourage all who read it to take up and enjoy a very exciting and challenging sport. Standards are rising daily, and the demand that will be placed on participants will require a keen dedication. The weightlifter is a complete athlete and this is a sport, unlike so many others, in which participation can continue over many years. To do real justice to yourself you should join a good club. Most towns and cities in Britain sport a weightlifting club, and there are excellent facilities at the new sports centres that are being built throughout Britain. For the younger lifter many schools now include weightlifting as an important part of their sports curriculum.

There are many fine clubs with very good coaches just wanting to help you. Check with the British Amateur Weightlifters Association and accept the challenge of being one of Britain's Strongest Men!

Important Addresses in Weightlifting

B.A.W.L.A. General Secretary and Coaching Secretary
W. W. R. Holland, 3 Iffley Turn, Oxford.

B.A.W.L.A. Schools Secretary
D. Mulkerrin, 36 Amesbury Road, Hanworth, Middlesex.

Schoolboys Award Scheme Registrar
H. Price, 35 Lynn Road, Terrington St. Clement, Kings Lynn, Norfolk.

B.A.W.L.A. Championships Secretary
H. Binder, 42 Thirlemere Road, Muswell Hill, London N10.

B.A.W.L.A. National Coach
J. Lear, The Willows, 4 Fords Heath, Shrewsbury, Shropshire.

For details of Divisions of the B.A.W.L.A. and all clubs, contact the B.A.W.L.A. Secretary—W. W. R. Holland.

Acknowledgments
A. Murray—National Coaching Adviser B.A.W.L.A.
O. State O.B.E.—Photographs.
G. Kirkley—Photographs (Strength Athlete).